The History

Unraveling the Enigma of the Frozen Continent

Copyright © 2023 by Scott Ernest Nansen and Einar Felix Hansen.

All rights reserved. No part of this publication may be reproduced, stored in a retrieval system, or transmitted, in any form or by any means, electronic, mechanical, photocopying, recording, or otherwise, without the prior written permission of the copyright holder. This book was created with the help of Artificial Intelligence technology.

The contents of this book are intended for entertainment purposes only. While every effort has been made to ensure the accuracy and reliability of the information presented, the author and publisher make no warranties or representations as to the accuracy, completeness, or suitability of the information contained herein. The information presented in this book is not intended as a substitute for professional advice, and readers should consult with qualified professionals in the relevant fields for specific advice.

Introduction: The Icy Continent of Antarctica 5

The Geological History of Antarctica: From Gondwana to Today 8

Early Human Encounters with Antarctica: Myth and Legend 11

The First Recorded Sighting of Antarctica: The Age of Exploration Begins 13

The Race to the South Pole: Amundsen and Scott 15

Whaling in the Southern Ocean: The Golden Age of Antarctic Exploitation 18

The Discovery of Antarctica's Interior: The Heroic Age of Antarctic Exploration 20

The Role of Science in Antarctic Exploration: Mapping and Research 22

The Falkland Islands War: The Battle for South Georgia 24

The Antarctic Treaty System: An International Agreement for the Frozen Continent 26

Cold War Politics in Antarctica: The Race for Strategic Advantage 28

Antarctic Wildlife: From Penguins to Whales 30

Antarctic Oceanography: Studying the Southern Ocean 32

The First Overwintering Expeditions: Surviving the Antarctic Winter 34

Shackleton's Endurance Expedition: A Tale of Survival and Leadership 36

Antarctica During World War II: Military Operations and Scientific Research 38

Ancient Climate Change in Antarctica: Evidence from Ice Cores 40

The Ross Ice Shelf: A History of Exploration and Scientific Discovery 42

The Search for Meteorites in Antarctica: Studying the Origin of the Solar System 44

Medieval Maps and the Idea of Terra Australis Incognita: The Imaginary Continent of the South 46

The Piri Reis Map and the Mystery of Antarctica: Did Ancient Mariners Discover the Continent? 48

Ancient Artifacts and Structures in Antarctica: Evidence of a Forgotten Civilization? 50

The History of Antarctic Fiction: From Edgar Allan Poe to John Carpenter 52

The Future of Antarctica: Balancing Environmental Protection and Resource Development 54

Conclusion 56

Introduction: The Icy Continent of Antarctica

The southernmost continent on Earth, Antarctica is a vast and frozen wilderness that has fascinated explorers, scientists, and adventurers for centuries. It is a land of towering ice cliffs, piercingly cold winds, and a stark beauty that is both awe-inspiring and unforgiving. In this chapter, we will explore the geography, climate, and history of this icy continent, and delve into the many mysteries and marvels that make it such a unique and captivating place.

Antarctica is a continent like no other. Located at the southern pole of the Earth, it is the fifth-largest continent in terms of land area, and is roughly twice the size of Australia. However, unlike other continents, Antarctica is almost entirely covered by ice, with ice sheets that are up to 4.7 kilometers (2.9 miles) thick in some places. The ice sheets of Antarctica hold more than 90% of the world's fresh water, making it an incredibly important and unique resource.

The geography of Antarctica is defined by its ice, which shapes the landscape in a way that is both stunning and unforgiving. Massive glaciers flow down from the high plateaus, carving out deep valleys and fjords in the ice. The coastline is dotted with towering ice cliffs that can rise up to 100 meters (328 feet) above sea level. Inland, the terrain is a vast and undulating sea of ice, with occasional mountains and nunataks (isolated peaks) jutting up from the frozen expanse.

The climate of Antarctica is one of the harshest on Earth. The continent is located at the south pole, which means that it receives almost no direct sunlight for six months of the year. During this time, the temperature can drop to as low as -89°C (-128°F), making it the coldest place on Earth. Even during the summer months, the temperature rarely rises above freezing, and the wind can gust to hurricane force, creating blizzards that can last for days.

Despite its harsh climate and inhospitable terrain, Antarctica is home to a surprising variety of life. Penguins, seals, and seabirds thrive in the waters around the continent, while mosses, lichens, and other hardy plants cling to the rocky outcrops and ice-free areas. Marine mammals such as whales and dolphins can also be found in the waters around Antarctica.

The history of Antarctica is as fascinating as its geography and climate. For centuries, the continent was known only by rumor and legend, with ancient maps depicting a vast and unknown southern land called Terra Australis Incognita. It wasn't until the 19th century that explorers began to make serious attempts to reach the continent, and even then, their efforts were often fraught with danger and hardship.

In the early 20th century, the race to the South Pole captured the world's attention, as explorers such as Roald Amundsen and Robert Falcon Scott battled it out to be the first to reach the pole. The Heroic Age of Antarctic Exploration saw many other expeditions to the continent, as explorers sought to map the interior, study the wildlife, and unlock the secrets of this icy wilderness.

Today, Antarctica is a place of scientific research, with dozens of research stations scattered across the continent. Scientists study everything from climate change and geology to astrophysics and marine biology, using the continent's unique environment to gain insights into the workings of the planet and the universe.

In this book, we will explore the history of Antarctica in depth, from the ancient myths and legends to the modern-day scientific expeditions. We will delve into the challenges and triumphs of the explorers, the mysteries and marvels of the continent's geography and wildlife, and the complex issues surrounding environmental protection and resource development. We will also examine the impact of human activities on Antarctica, from the exploitation of its natural resources to the effects of climate change and pollution.

Throughout this book, we will see that Antarctica is much more than just a frozen wasteland; it is a place of extraordinary beauty, complexity, and significance. Its unique geology, climate, and wildlife offer insights into the history of our planet and the workings of the natural world, while its exploration and scientific research provide a window into the ingenuity, resilience, and curiosity of the human spirit.

As we embark on this journey through the history of Antarctica, we will discover a place that is both familiar and foreign, and that challenges us to rethink our place in the world and our relationship with the environment. So come with me as we explore the icy continent of Antarctica, and discover the wonders and mysteries that lie hidden beneath its frozen surface.

The Geological History of Antarctica: From Gondwana to Today

Antarctica's geological history stretches back over 4 billion years, and is intertwined with the history of the supercontinent Gondwana, which once included Antarctica, Africa, South America, Australia, India, and Antarctica. In this chapter, we will explore the geological history of Antarctica, from its formation as part of Gondwana to the present day, and learn about the fascinating processes that shaped this icy continent.

Antarctica was not always the frozen continent we know today. In fact, during the early Paleozoic era (around 540 million years ago), it was located near the equator, and was covered by a shallow, tropical sea. This period is known as the Cambrian period, and it was during this time that the first forms of complex life emerged on Earth.

Over the next several hundred million years, Antarctica slowly drifted southward, away from the equator. By the time the supercontinent Gondwana began to form around 600 million years ago, Antarctica was located near the southern pole. Gondwana was a massive landmass that included most of the southern hemisphere, and it was during this time that Antarctica began to take on its current shape and geography.

During the Paleozoic era, which lasted from around 540 million to 250 million years ago, Antarctica was home to a diverse array of plant and animal life. Fossil evidence from this era shows that the continent was covered in lush forests and swamps, and was inhabited by a variety of amphibians, reptiles, and early mammals. However, by the end of the Paleozoic era, around 250 million years ago, a mass extinction wiped out much of the life on Earth, and Antarctica began to shift from a land of forests and swamps to a frozen wasteland.

The Mesozoic era, which lasted from around 250 million to 66 million years ago, saw the emergence of the dinosaurs, as well as the formation of the supercontinent Pangea. Antarctica was located near the South Pole during this time, and was covered in ice and snow. However, fossil evidence shows that some dinosaurs were able to survive in Antarctica's relatively mild coastal regions, which were not as cold and inhospitable as the interior.

Around 100 million years ago, Pangea began to break up, and Gondwana began to split into the continents we know today. Antarctica separated from South America around 35 million years ago, and has been isolated from the other continents ever since. As a result, it has developed a unique array of flora and fauna, and has been the subject of intense scientific study for decades.

The most significant geological event in Antarctica's recent history has been the formation of its massive ice sheets, which began to form around 35 million years ago. These ice sheets grew in size and thickness over millions of years, and today cover almost the entire continent. The ice sheets are up to 4.7 kilometers (2.9 miles) thick in some places, and hold more than 90% of the world's fresh water.

Antarctica's geology is also shaped by its location at the edge of the tectonic plates that make up the Earth's crust. The continent sits on the boundary between the Antarctic Plate and the South American Plate, and is home to a number of active volcanoes, including Mount Erebus, which is the southernmost active volcano on Earth.

In recent years, scientists have used ice cores drilled from Antarctica's ice sheets to learn more about the continent's geological history. These ice cores contain records of past climate conditions, as well as evidence of volcanic eruptions, atmospheric pollution, and other phenomena.

Overall, the geological history of Antarctica is a story of incredible transformation and adaptation. From its origins as a tropical sea, to its current status as a frozen wilderness, Antarctica has undergone countless changes over the course of billions of years. And yet, despite its harsh climate and inhospitable terrain, life has managed to thrive on this icy continent, adapting to its unique conditions and leaving behind a rich and fascinating fossil record.

Today, Antarctica remains a crucial site for scientific research, offering insights into the workings of the planet and the universe. The continent's unique geology and climate make it an ideal place to study everything from climate change and astrophysics to marine biology and geology. And as we continue to explore and learn about Antarctica's geological history, we are sure to discover even more marvels and mysteries hidden beneath its frozen surface.

Early Human Encounters with Antarctica: Myth and Legend

For centuries, Antarctica remained an unknown and mysterious land, hidden behind a veil of ice and snow. However, even before the continent was officially discovered by European explorers, there were tales and legends of a great southern land that lay beyond the seas. In this chapter, we will explore the myths and legends surrounding Antarctica, and learn about the early human encounters with this enigmatic continent.

Many ancient cultures had stories and myths about a distant southern land, which was said to be a place of great riches and wonder. In ancient Greek mythology, the land of Hyperborea was said to be located beyond the north wind, while in Hindu mythology, the land of Jambudvipa was said to be located beyond the southern ocean.

One of the earliest known references to Antarctica can be found in the work of the ancient Greek philosopher Aristotle, who speculated that there must be a landmass in the southern hemisphere to balance out the land in the northern hemisphere. However, it wasn't until the Middle Ages that the idea of a southern continent began to take hold in the popular imagination.

Medieval maps often depicted a vast and unknown southern land called Terra Australis Incognita, which was said to be a land of great wealth and adventure. The concept of Terra Australis was first proposed by the ancient Greeks, but it wasn't until the 16th century that European explorers began to make serious attempts to reach this fabled land.

One of the earliest known European encounters with Antarctica was the voyage of the Portuguese explorer Vasco da Gama in 1497. Da Gama sailed along the coast of Africa and into the Indian Ocean, and is said to have sighted the coast of Antarctica, although there is little evidence to support this claim.

Another early explorer who is said to have encountered Antarctica was the Dutch navigator Willem Janszoon. In 1606, Janszoon sailed into the Gulf of Carpentaria in northern Australia, and claimed to have seen a large landmass to the south, which he called "Land van Papegay" (Parrot Land).

It wasn't until the 18th century that the first confirmed sightings of Antarctica were made. In 1773, the British explorer James Cook sailed into the Antarctic Circle, becoming the first European to do so. Cook's voyages helped to dispel many of the myths and legends surrounding Antarctica, and laid the groundwork for future exploration and discovery. Despite these early encounters, Antarctica remained a largely unexplored and unknown land until the 19th century. It was during this time that the race to reach the South Pole began, and explorers such as Roald Amundsen and Robert Falcon Scott set out to conquer the icy wilderness.

Today, Antarctica remains a place of fascination and wonder, inspiring scientists, explorers, and adventurers from around the world. And while the myths and legends surrounding this enigmatic continent may have been dispelled, its mysteries and marvels continue to captivate us, reminding us of the enduring power of the human imagination.

The First Recorded Sighting of Antarctica: The Age of Exploration Begins

The first recorded sighting of Antarctica is a story of adventure, perseverance, and discovery. For centuries, sailors and explorers had speculated about the existence of a great southern land, but it wasn't until the 18th century that the first confirmed sighting of the continent was made. In this chapter, we will explore the history of the first recorded sighting of Antarctica, and learn about the explorers who braved the icy waters of the southern ocean in search of adventure and discovery.

The first recorded sighting of Antarctica is credited to the Russian explorer Fabian Gottlieb von Bellingshausen, who led an expedition to the southern ocean in 1819-1821. Bellingshausen was a veteran of the Russian navy, and had previously sailed with Captain James Cook on his second voyage to the Pacific. In July of 1819, Bellingshausen set out from Rio de Janeiro, Brazil, aboard the ships Vostok and Mirny. His goal was to explore the southern ocean and find new lands for the Russian empire. Over the next several months, Bellingshausen and his crew encountered icebergs, storms, and treacherous seas, but they persevered, pushing farther and farther south in search of new discoveries.

On January 27, 1820, Bellingshausen and his crew became the first known humans to lay eyes on the continent of Antarctica. They spotted land on the horizon, and as they approached, they saw towering ice cliffs and glaciers stretching as far as the eye could see. Bellingshausen named the land "The Southern Thule," and claimed it for the Russian empire.

Over the next several weeks, Bellingshausen and his crew continued to explore the waters around Antarctica, mapping the coastline and collecting specimens of plants and animals. They also encountered several other ships, including the British explorer Edward Bransfield, who is credited with making the first confirmed landing on the continent just three days after Bellingshausen's sighting.

Bellingshausen's expedition was a significant milestone in the history of Antarctic exploration, and helped to lay the groundwork for future expeditions and discoveries. His observations and maps provided valuable insights into the geography and geology of the continent, and helped to dispel many of the myths and legends that had surrounded Antarctica for centuries. Today, Bellingshausen's achievement is celebrated as a symbol of human ingenuity, courage, and perseverance. It is a reminder of the power of exploration and discovery, and of the enduring spirit of adventure that has driven humans to explore the farthest reaches of the planet and beyond.

The first recorded sighting of Antarctica marked the beginning of the age of exploration, and set in motion a series of expeditions and discoveries that would transform our understanding of the world and ourselves. From Bellingshausen's daring voyage to the heroic expeditions of Scott, Amundsen, and Shackleton, the story of Antarctic exploration is a testament to the resilience, bravery, and curiosity of the human spirit. And as we continue to explore and learn about this frozen continent, we are sure to discover even more wonders and mysteries hidden beneath its icy surface.

The Race to the South Pole: Amundsen and Scott

The race to the South Pole is one of the most iconic stories in the history of Antarctic exploration. It was a tale of bravery, determination, and endurance, as two teams of explorers battled against the harsh and unforgiving conditions of the southern continent to reach the southernmost point on Earth. In this chapter, we will explore the story of the race to the South Pole, and learn about the two explorers who led their teams to this incredible achievement: Roald Amundsen and Robert Falcon Scott.

Roald Amundsen was a Norwegian explorer who had already achieved several notable feats of exploration before he set his sights on the South Pole. In 1903-1906, he had become the first person to sail through the Northwest Passage, and in 1910-1912, he had led an expedition to the Antarctic, during which he became the first person to sail across the Antarctic Circle.

Robert Falcon Scott was a British naval officer who had also been involved in previous expeditions to the Antarctic. In 1901-1904, he had led the Discovery expedition, during which he had explored the Ross Sea region of Antarctica. However, he was determined to be the first person to reach the South Pole, and in 1910, he set out on his second expedition to the southern continent.

The race to the South Pole began in earnest in the summer of 1911, when both Amundsen and Scott set out from their base camps on the edge of the Ross Ice Shelf. Amundsen's team consisted of five men and 52 dogs, while Scott's team consisted of 17 men and a team of ponies, motor sledges, and dogs.

Over the next several months, both teams battled against extreme cold, high winds, and treacherous terrain, as they made their way across the ice and snow of the southern continent. Amundsen's team took a more direct route to the pole, following a path along the Ross Ice Shelf and then heading inland towards the pole. Scott's team took a more circuitous route, following the path of previous expeditions to the Ross Sea, before turning inland towards the pole.

On December 14, 1911, Amundsen's team reached the South Pole, becoming the first people in history to stand at the southernmost point on Earth. They planted the Norwegian flag, and spent several days exploring the area and taking measurements.

Scott's team arrived at the South Pole several weeks later, on January 17, 1912, only to discover that Amundsen's team had beaten them to the pole. Scott and his team were devastated by the news, but they continued to press on, determined to complete their mission.

Tragically, however, Scott and his team never made it back to their base camp. They were caught in a blizzard on their return journey, and all five members of the polar party perished. Their bodies were discovered eight months later, and their deaths became one of the most poignant stories in the history of Antarctic exploration.

The race to the South Pole was a triumph of human endurance and exploration, but it also revealed the dangers and challenges of exploring the southern continent. Both

Amundsen and Scott had to contend with extreme cold, harsh winds, and treacherous terrain, and both faced the very real risk of death at every turn.

Today, the legacy of the race to the South Pole lives on, inspiring new generations of explorers, adventurers, and scientists. And as we continue to explore and learn about this frozen continent, we are sure to discover even more wonders and mysteries hidden beneath its icy surface.

Whaling in the Southern Ocean: The Golden Age of Antarctic Exploitation

For nearly two centuries, the southern ocean was a hunting ground for whalers, who sought out the huge populations of whales that thrived in the icy waters around Antarctica. The whaling industry brought wealth and prosperity to many countries, but it also had a devastating impact on the environment and the marine life of the southern ocean. In this chapter, we will explore the history of whaling in the southern ocean, and learn about the impact of this industry on the fragile ecosystem of Antarctica.

Whaling in the southern ocean began in earnest in the early 19th century, as the demand for whale oil and other products grew around the world. The waters around Antarctica were home to vast populations of whales, including the humpback, blue, and sperm whales, which were prized for their oil, blubber, and bone.

Whaling ships from many countries, including the United States, Britain, France, and Norway, made their way to the southern ocean, where they hunted whales using a variety of methods. Some used harpoons fired from small boats, while others used explosive-tipped harpoons fired from the decks of the whaling ships themselves.

The whaling industry was a lucrative one, and it brought wealth and prosperity to many countries. However, it also had a devastating impact on the environment and the marine life of the southern ocean. Over the course of several decades, the whale populations in the southern ocean were decimated, with many species pushed to the brink of extinction.

In addition to the impact on whale populations, whaling also had a significant impact on the fragile ecosystem of Antarctica. Whaling ships often dumped large amounts of waste and pollution into the waters, and their presence disrupted the natural balance of the ecosystem.

Despite the devastating impact of whaling on the southern ocean, the industry continued for many years, with new technology and methods allowing for even more efficient and ruthless hunting of whales. It wasn't until the mid-20th century that the global community began to take action to protect the whale populations of the southern ocean.

Today, whaling in the southern ocean is largely banned, with many countries and international organizations working to protect the fragile ecosystem of Antarctica and the marine life that calls it home. However, the legacy of the whaling industry remains, a reminder of the dangers of exploiting the natural world without regard for the consequences.

Whaling in the southern ocean was a dark chapter in the history of Antarctic exploration, one that reminds us of the importance of responsible and sustainable stewardship of the planet. As we continue to explore and learn about the frozen continent of Antarctica, we must do so with a deep respect for the delicate balance of its ecosystems, and a commitment to preserving its wonders and mysteries for generations to come.

The Discovery of Antarctica's Interior: The Heroic Age of Antarctic Exploration

The discovery of Antarctica's interior is a story of courage, determination, and sacrifice. In the early 20th century, a new generation of explorers set out to conquer the frozen continent, braving extreme cold, high winds, and treacherous terrain in their quest to unlock the secrets of this enigmatic land. In this chapter, we will explore the history of the heroic age of Antarctic exploration, and learn about the explorers who made some of the most significant discoveries in the continent's history.

The heroic age of Antarctic exploration began in the early 20th century, as a new wave of explorers set out to unlock the secrets of the southern continent. Among the most famous of these explorers were Robert Falcon Scott, Ernest Shackleton, and Roald Amundsen, all of whom sought to make new discoveries and achieve new feats of exploration and endurance.

One of the most significant discoveries of the heroic age of Antarctic exploration was the discovery of the polar plateau, a vast expanse of ice and snow that stretches across the interior of the continent. This discovery was made by Scott and his team during the Terra Nova expedition of 1910-1913.

Scott's team, which included scientists, geologists, and other experts, set out from their base camp on the Ross Ice Shelf in the summer of 1911, with the goal of reaching the South Pole and making new discoveries along the way.

They faced extreme cold, harsh winds, and treacherous terrain, but they persevered, pushing farther and farther south into the unknown. In January of 1912, Scott and his team reached the South Pole, but they were devastated to discover that Roald Amundsen's team had beaten them there by several weeks. Despite this setback, Scott and his team continued to press on, making new discoveries and mapping the interior of the continent.

One of the most significant discoveries made by Scott's team was the discovery of the polar plateau, a vast expanse of ice and snow that stretches across the interior of the continent. This discovery was a major milestone in the history of Antarctic exploration, and opened up new avenues for scientific research and exploration.

The heroic age of Antarctic exploration was a time of incredible achievement and discovery, but it was also a time of great sacrifice and tragedy. In 1914, Ernest Shackleton set out on an expedition to cross the continent from one side to the other, but his ship, the Endurance, became trapped in ice and was eventually crushed. Shackleton and his team were forced to survive for months in the harsh Antarctic wilderness, enduring extreme cold, hunger, and isolation, before being rescued by a daring rescue mission.

Despite the dangers and challenges of Antarctic exploration, the heroic age of exploration opened up new frontiers of knowledge and discovery, and inspired new generations of explorers and adventurers. Today, Antarctica remains a place of fascination and wonder, offering insights into the workings of the planet and the universe, and reminding us of the enduring power of human curiosity and ingenuity.

The Role of Science in Antarctic Exploration: Mapping and Research

While exploration and adventure have long been the hallmarks of Antarctic exploration, the role of science has also been a crucial part of the continent's history. From mapping and surveying to studying the climate and geology of the region, scientific research has played a vital role in unlocking the secrets of this frozen land. In this chapter, we will explore the role of science in Antarctic exploration, and learn about the groundbreaking research that has taken place on the continent.

The scientific exploration of Antarctica began in earnest in the early 20th century, with the establishment of research stations and the deployment of scientific expeditions to the continent. Among the most important of these early expeditions was the British National Antarctic Expedition of 1901-1904, which included a team of scientists and researchers led by Robert Falcon Scott.

Scott's team conducted extensive research in the region, including mapping and surveying of the coast and interior, collecting specimens of plants and animals, and studying the geology and climate of the region. Their work laid the foundation for future scientific expeditions to the continent, and helped to establish Antarctica as a major center for scientific research and discovery.

Over the years, a wide range of scientific research has taken place on the continent, with researchers from around the world studying everything from the formation of the continent to the behavior of its wildlife. Some of the most significant scientific discoveries made in Antarctica include the discovery of the ozone hole in the 1980s, and the discovery of new species of plants and animals that are found nowhere else on Earth.

In addition to its scientific research, Antarctica also plays a critical role in understanding the broader workings of the planet and the universe. The continent's extreme environment and isolation make it an ideal place for studying topics like climate change, geology, and astronomy. Researchers have used Antarctica as a platform for studying everything from the behavior of the sun to the formation of the universe itself.

Today, Antarctica remains a vital center for scientific research and discovery, with research stations and expeditions from countries around the world studying a wide range of topics. Advances in technology and communication have made it easier than ever for researchers to collaborate and share their findings, making Antarctica a hub of scientific knowledge and discovery.

The role of science in Antarctic exploration has been critical to our understanding of the continent and its place in the wider world. From mapping and surveying to groundbreaking discoveries in fields like astronomy and climate science, the research that has taken place on the continent has helped to unlock the secrets of this frozen land, and provide new insights into the workings of the planet and the universe.

The Falkland Islands War: The Battle for South Georgia

The Falkland Islands War, also known as the Falklands War, was a conflict that took place in 1982 between Argentina and the United Kingdom over the disputed Falkland Islands in the South Atlantic. The war was a major turning point in the history of the region, and had a significant impact on the political and strategic balance of power in the Southern Hemisphere. In this chapter, we will explore the Battle for South Georgia, a key conflict in the Falklands War, and learn about the events that led up to the conflict, the strategies and tactics used by the opposing forces, and the aftermath of the conflict.

The Falkland Islands, a British overseas territory in the South Atlantic, had been a source of tension between Argentina and the UK for many years. Argentina had long claimed sovereignty over the islands, which it called the Malvinas, and had made several attempts to establish its control over the islands, including a failed invasion in 1966.

In 1982, tensions between Argentina and the UK reached a boiling point, and Argentina launched a surprise invasion of the Falkland Islands. The UK responded with a military task force, which set sail for the South Atlantic to retake the islands.

One of the key conflicts in the Falklands War was the Battle for South Georgia, a remote island near the southern tip of South America. The island had been seized by

Argentine forces in March 1982, and was seen as a key strategic target for the UK.

The UK launched a naval task force to retake South Georgia, which was met by a smaller Argentine force. The two sides engaged in a brief but intense battle, with the UK ultimately emerging victorious. The Battle for South Georgia was a critical turning point in the Falklands War, demonstrating the UK's military prowess and its determination to retake the islands.

The conflict in the Falklands was marked by a number of notable strategies and tactics on both sides. The Argentine military relied heavily on surprise attacks and unconventional tactics, while the UK deployed advanced weaponry and tactics, including the use of special forces and air power.

The aftermath of the Falklands War was significant, with the conflict leading to the deaths of hundreds of soldiers and civilians on both sides, as well as causing significant political and strategic changes in the region. The conflict also highlighted the importance of international law and diplomacy in resolving territorial disputes, and led to renewed efforts by both Argentina and the UK to find a peaceful resolution to the long-standing dispute over the Falkland Islands.

The Battle for South Georgia was a critical conflict in the Falklands War, demonstrating the military capabilities of both sides, and ultimately leading to a decisive victory for the UK. The conflict was a sobering reminder of the dangers and costs of war, and highlighted the importance of diplomacy and international cooperation in resolving disputes and preventing conflict.

The Antarctic Treaty System: An International Agreement for the Frozen Continent

The Antarctic Treaty System is a remarkable international agreement that has helped to preserve and protect the continent of Antarctica for nearly 60 years. The treaty, which was signed in 1959, is a model of international cooperation and diplomacy, and has been instrumental in establishing Antarctica as a unique and valuable scientific research and exploration site. In this chapter, we will explore the history and significance of the Antarctic Treaty System, and learn about its key provisions and the impact it has had on the continent.

The Antarctic Treaty System was signed in Washington D.C. in 1959 by 12 countries, including the United States, the United Kingdom, Australia, and the Soviet Union. The treaty was designed to ensure that Antarctica remained a peaceful and cooperative scientific research site, and to promote the protection of the continent's unique and fragile ecosystem.

Under the terms of the treaty, Antarctica is designated as a demilitarized zone, with all military activity strictly prohibited. The treaty also establishes guidelines for scientific research and exploration, and sets out protocols for the protection of the continent's wildlife and environment.

One of the key provisions of the Antarctic Treaty System is the establishment of the Committee for Environmental Protection, which is responsible for overseeing and enforcing the environmental protocols established under the treaty. The committee is made up of representatives from all signatory nations, and works to ensure that all activities on the continent are conducted in a manner that is sustainable and respectful of the delicate ecosystem.

The Antarctic Treaty System has been remarkably successful in achieving its goals of preserving and protecting the continent of Antarctica. Over the years, the treaty has been expanded to include additional provisions and protocols, including the Madrid Protocol, which designates Antarctica as a natural reserve and prohibits all mining activity on the continent.

The treaty has also been a model of international cooperation and diplomacy, with signatory nations working together to address common challenges and to promote the scientific and environmental goals of the treaty. The treaty has served as a beacon of hope for international cooperation in the face of global challenges, and has demonstrated that even in the most extreme environments, cooperation and collaboration are possible.

The Antarctic Treaty System has had a profound impact on the continent of Antarctica, helping to establish it as a unique and valuable scientific research and exploration site, and promoting the protection of its fragile and unique ecosystem. As we continue to explore and learn about the frozen continent, we must do so with a deep respect for the principles of the Antarctic Treaty System, and a commitment to preserving its wonders and mysteries for generations to come.

Cold War Politics in Antarctica: The Race for Strategic Advantage

During the Cold War, the continent of Antarctica became a key battleground for political and strategic advantage between the United States and the Soviet Union. Both countries recognized the importance of Antarctica as a potential military outpost and strategic location, and worked to establish research stations and conduct scientific research on the continent. In this chapter, we will explore the history of Cold War politics in Antarctica, and learn about the strategies and tactics used by both sides to gain a foothold on the frozen continent.

The Cold War was a time of intense political and military competition between the United States and the Soviet Union, with both sides seeking to gain strategic advantage over the other. Antarctica, with its remote and isolated location, was seen as a potential site for military installations and research facilities, and both sides worked to establish a presence on the continent.

The US and the Soviet Union both established research stations in Antarctica during the 1950s and 1960s, and conducted extensive scientific research in the region. These research stations were also used as a platform for gathering intelligence on the other side, with both sides using their scientific expeditions as cover for espionage activities.

One of the most significant events in the history of Cold War politics in Antarctica was the signing of the Antarctic Treaty System in 1959. The treaty, which established Antarctica as a demilitarized zone and designated it as a scientific research site, was seen as a critical victory for the US, which had been working to prevent the Soviet Union from gaining a foothold on the continent.

Despite the provisions of the Antarctic Treaty System, both sides continued to engage in military and strategic activities in Antarctica during the Cold War. The US conducted a number of secret military missions in the region, including the establishment of a nuclear-powered weather station in the late 1960s. The Soviet Union also conducted military and strategic activities on the continent, including the construction of a secret underground research facility in the late 1970s.

The end of the Cold War in the early 1990s marked a turning point in the history of Antarctica, with both the US and the Soviet Union scaling back their activities on the continent. Today, Antarctica remains a demilitarized zone, with scientific research and environmental protection serving as the primary focus of activity on the continent.

Cold War politics in Antarctica was a reflection of the larger geopolitical struggles of the time, with both the US and the Soviet Union seeking to gain strategic advantage and promote their interests on the frozen continent. Despite the tensions and conflicts of the time, however, the Antarctic Treaty System demonstrated the power of international cooperation and diplomacy, and helped to preserve Antarctica as a peaceful and cooperative research site for generations to come.

Antarctic Wildlife: From Penguins to Whales

Antarctica is home to a remarkable array of wildlife, including some of the most iconic and beloved species on the planet. From penguins and seals to whales and birds, the frozen continent is a veritable paradise for nature lovers and wildlife enthusiasts. In this chapter, we will explore the diverse and fascinating world of Antarctic wildlife, and learn about the unique adaptations and behaviors that allow these creatures to thrive in one of the harshest and most inhospitable environments on Earth.

Perhaps the most famous of all Antarctic wildlife are the penguins. These iconic birds are found throughout the continent, and are beloved for their comical waddling gait, distinctive black-and-white coloring, and quirky personalities. There are several species of penguin that make their homes in Antarctica, including the emperor penguin, which is the largest of all penguins, and the Adélie penguin, which is known for its playful and curious behavior.

Seals are another common sight in Antarctica, with several species calling the continent home. Weddell seals are perhaps the most famous of these, with their distinctive spotted fur and large size. Leopard seals, which are known for their fierce and predatory behavior, are also commonly found in Antarctic waters.

Whales are another important component of the Antarctic ecosystem, with several species of these majestic creatures calling the continent home. The southern right whale and the humpback whale are perhaps the most common of these, and can often be seen swimming in Antarctic waters or breaching the surface in spectacular displays.

Birds are also an important part of the Antarctic ecosystem, with several species making their homes on the continent. The snow petrel is perhaps the most iconic of these, with its pure white plumage and striking red eyes. Albatrosses, skuas, and terns are also commonly found in the region, and play important roles in the food chain and ecosystem of the continent.

Perhaps one of the most fascinating aspects of Antarctic wildlife is the unique adaptations and behaviors that allow these creatures to survive in such a harsh and inhospitable environment. From the thick layers of blubber that keep seals and whales warm in freezing waters, to the huddling behavior of penguins that helps them conserve heat, Antarctic wildlife has evolved a range of incredible strategies for surviving in one of the most extreme environments on the planet.

The diversity and beauty of Antarctic wildlife is a testament to the incredible resilience and adaptability of nature. From penguins and seals to whales and birds, the continent of Antarctica is home to a remarkable array of creatures that have captured the imaginations of people around the world. As we continue to explore and learn about this frozen land, we must do so with a deep respect for the unique and fragile ecosystem that supports these amazing creatures, and a commitment to protecting it for generations to come.

Antarctic Oceanography: Studying the Southern Ocean

The Southern Ocean, which surrounds Antarctica, is one of the most challenging and fascinating ocean environments on the planet. This vast and remote ocean is characterized by extreme conditions, including freezing temperatures, high winds, and massive waves, which have made it a difficult and dangerous place for humans to study. Despite these challenges, however, scientists have made remarkable progress in understanding the physical and biological processes that shape this unique and vital ecosystem. In this chapter, we will explore the world of Antarctic oceanography, and learn about the tools and techniques that scientists use to study the Southern Ocean.

One of the key challenges of studying the Southern Ocean is its remote and inaccessible location. The ocean is surrounded by the vast and inhospitable continent of Antarctica, which makes it difficult for scientists to access and study. In recent years, however, advances in technology and logistics have made it possible for scientists to conduct more extensive and sophisticated research in the region.

One of the primary tools used by Antarctic oceanographers is the research vessel, which is used to conduct surveys and collect data on the physical and biological properties of the ocean. These vessels are equipped with a range of instruments, including sensors and probes, which allow scientists to collect data on temperature, salinity, and other key oceanographic parameters.

Another important tool in the study of the Southern Ocean is remote sensing, which involves the use of satellite and other remote sensing technologies to gather data on ocean conditions. These technologies allow scientists to study large areas of the ocean at once, and to monitor changes in ocean conditions over time.

One of the key areas of research in Antarctic oceanography is the study of ocean currents and circulation patterns. The Southern Ocean is characterized by a complex and dynamic system of currents and eddies, which play a critical role in regulating the global climate and transporting nutrients and other materials throughout the ocean.

Another important area of research is the study of marine ecosystems and biodiversity. The Southern Ocean is home to a rich and diverse array of marine life, including krill, squid, and a variety of fish and other species. Scientists are working to understand the complex interactions between these species, as well as the impact of human activities on the fragile and unique ecosystem of the Southern Ocean.

Despite the challenges and difficulties of studying the Southern Ocean, Antarctic oceanography has made remarkable progress in recent years, providing valuable insights into the workings of one of the most important and unique ocean environments on the planet. As we continue to explore and learn about the Southern Ocean, it is critical that we work to protect and preserve this vital ecosystem, and to ensure that it remains a vibrant and healthy part of our planet for generations to come.

The First Overwintering Expeditions: Surviving the Antarctic Winter

The Antarctic winter is one of the harshest and most inhospitable environments on the planet, with extreme temperatures, high winds, and limited daylight. Despite these challenges, however, humans have been living and working in Antarctica for over a century, with scientists and explorers braving the long, dark winter months in order to conduct research and exploration on the frozen continent. In this chapter, we will explore the history of overwintering in Antarctica, and learn about the strategies and tactics used by early expeditions to survive in this challenging and unforgiving environment.

The first overwintering expedition to Antarctica took place in 1898, when a team led by Belgian explorer Adrien de Gerlache spent the winter months at Cape Adare, on the coast of Antarctica. The team faced a range of challenges during their stay, including isolation, harsh weather, and limited supplies, but managed to survive and conduct a range of scientific research and exploration activities.

Over the next several decades, numerous expeditions would brave the Antarctic winter, including the famous British expeditions led by Robert Falcon Scott and Ernest Shackleton. These expeditions faced a range of challenges, including scurvy, frostbite, and mental health issues caused by the extreme isolation and confinement of winter life in Antarctica.

One of the key strategies used by early overwintering expeditions was to establish a routine and structure to daily life. This involved establishing regular work and sleep schedules, as well as engaging in a range of recreational and social activities to help maintain morale and mental health. Many expeditions also made use of various forms of entertainment, including music, theater, and sports, to help break up the monotony of winter life in Antarctica.

Another important strategy used by overwintering expeditions was to maintain a steady supply of food and other essential resources. This involved careful planning and management of supplies, as well as the establishment of hunting and fishing programs to provide fresh food during the winter months.

Perhaps one of the most important factors in the success of overwintering expeditions in Antarctica was the strong sense of camaraderie and teamwork that developed among team members. In the face of extreme challenges and adversity, members of overwintering expeditions relied on each other for support and companionship, and developed deep bonds that lasted long after their return from the frozen continent.

The history of overwintering in Antarctica is a testament to the strength and resilience of the human spirit, and to the ingenuity and resourcefulness of those who have braved the harsh and unforgiving conditions of the Antarctic winter. As we continue to explore and learn about this remarkable continent, we must do so with a deep respect for the incredible feats of endurance and courage accomplished by those who came before us, and a commitment to preserving and protecting this unique and fragile ecosystem for generations to come.

Shackleton's Endurance Expedition: A Tale of Survival and Leadership

Ernest Shackleton's Endurance expedition is one of the most remarkable tales of survival and leadership in the history of Antarctic exploration. The expedition, which set out in 1914 with the goal of crossing the continent of Antarctica on foot, quickly became a struggle for survival as the expedition ship became trapped in ice and ultimately sank. Despite the many challenges and setbacks faced by the expedition, however, Shackleton's leadership and determination helped to ensure the survival of all members of the team. In this chapter, we will explore the history of Shackleton's Endurance expedition, and learn about the leadership lessons and survival strategies that can be drawn from this remarkable story.

The Endurance expedition set out from South Georgia Island in December 1914, with the goal of crossing the continent of Antarctica on foot. The expedition ship, the Endurance, became trapped in ice in the Weddell Sea in January 1915, and ultimately sank after several months of being crushed and battered by the ice.

Despite the loss of their ship, Shackleton and his crew refused to give up, and instead turned their focus to survival. The team established a camp on the ice floes, and worked to maintain a steady supply of food and water, as well as to preserve their physical and mental health in the face of extreme isolation and hardship.

One of the key factors in the success of the Endurance expedition was Shackleton's leadership and determination.

Shackleton was known for his ability to remain calm and focused in the face of adversity, and for his ability to inspire and motivate his team members. Despite the many challenges and setbacks faced by the expedition, Shackleton remained committed to the safety and well-being of his team, and worked tirelessly to ensure their survival.

Another important factor in the success of the Endurance expedition was the strong sense of teamwork and camaraderie that developed among team members. Despite the extreme isolation and hardship of their situation, team members worked together to support and encourage each other, and to maintain a positive and determined attitude.

The Endurance expedition also provides valuable lessons on survival and leadership that are relevant in a wide range of settings. Shackleton's ability to remain calm and focused under extreme pressure, his commitment to the safety and well-being of his team, and his ability to inspire and motivate his team members are all key qualities of effective leadership. The team's focus on maintaining a steady supply of food and water, and on preserving their physical and mental health, also provides valuable insights into the strategies and tactics necessary for survival in extreme environments.

The story of Shackleton's Endurance expedition is a remarkable testament to the power of leadership, teamwork, and determination in the face of extreme adversity. As we continue to explore and learn about the frozen continent of Antarctica, we can draw inspiration and valuable insights from this remarkable story of survival and leadership.

Antarctica During World War II: Military Operations and Scientific Research

Antarctica played an unexpected role in World War II, with both Allied and Axis powers conducting military operations and scientific research on the frozen continent. While Antarctica was far removed from the main theaters of the war, its strategic location and unique environment made it an important area of interest for military and scientific leaders on both sides. In this chapter, we will explore the history of Antarctica during World War II, and learn about the military operations and scientific research conducted by the various powers involved.

One of the key military operations in Antarctica during World War II was the British Operation Tabarin. This operation was established in 1943 with the goal of establishing a British presence in Antarctica, and involved the establishment of a number of research stations and military outposts throughout the continent. The operation played an important role in monitoring enemy activities in the region, and in providing a strategic foothold for Allied forces in the southern hemisphere.

Axis powers also had a significant presence in Antarctica during World War II, with both Germany and Japan conducting scientific research and exploration in the region. The German New Swabia expedition, for example, was a major scientific expedition led by the Nazi regime in 1938-1939, and involved the establishment of a number of research stations and scientific outposts throughout Antarctica. The Japanese also conducted a number of scientific expeditions in the region during the war, with a particular focus on the study of oceanography and marine biology.

Despite the military activities in Antarctica during World War II, scientific research also played an important role in the region during this time. The harsh and isolated environment of Antarctica provided a unique opportunity for scientists to conduct research in a range of fields, including geology, oceanography, and meteorology. Many of the research stations established during this time, such as the British base at Halley Bay and the American base at Little America, would go on to become important centers of scientific research and exploration for decades to come.

The history of Antarctica during World War II is a fascinating and complex chapter in the story of this unique continent. While military operations and scientific research were both conducted in the region during this time, the legacy of these activities continues to shape our understanding of Antarctica and its place in the world. As we continue to explore and learn about this remarkable land, it is important that we approach it with a deep respect for its complex and multifaceted history, and a commitment to preserving and protecting its unique and fragile ecosystem for future generations.

Ancient Climate Change in Antarctica: Evidence from Ice Cores

Antarctica is home to some of the largest and oldest ice sheets on the planet, with ice covering more than 98% of the continent. The ice sheets are not just an important feature of the Antarctic landscape, but also provide a record of ancient climate change stretching back hundreds of thousands of years. In this chapter, we will explore the history of climate change in Antarctica, and learn about the evidence for ancient climate change that has been uncovered through the study of ice cores.

Ice cores are long cylinders of ice drilled from the ice sheets of Antarctica, with each layer of ice representing a snapshot of the environment at the time it was formed. By studying these layers, scientists can learn about changes in temperature, atmospheric composition, and other key aspects of the climate over long periods of time.

One of the most significant findings from the study of ice cores is that the Earth's climate has varied widely over the past several hundred thousand years. The ice cores reveal that the Earth has experienced multiple ice ages, during which vast areas of the planet were covered in ice, as well as warmer interglacial periods during which ice sheets retreated and sea levels rose.

The study of ice cores has also provided valuable insights into the causes of climate change. For example, scientists have been able to measure levels of carbon dioxide and other greenhouse gases in ancient air bubbles trapped in the ice, revealing that atmospheric concentrations of these gases have fluctuated widely over time. This evidence supports the hypothesis that changes in atmospheric composition, driven in part by human activities such as burning of fossil fuels, are contributing to current global warming.

The study of ice cores has also revealed the impact of natural events such as volcanic eruptions and changes in solar activity on the Earth's climate. For example, evidence from ice cores indicates that a massive volcanic eruption around 74,000 years ago caused a significant cooling of the planet that lasted for several centuries.

The study of ancient climate change in Antarctica is a fascinating and important field of research, with implications for our understanding of the past, present, and future of the planet. As we continue to study and explore this unique continent, it is important that we continue to use the insights provided by ice cores and other tools to better understand the complex and dynamic systems that shape our planet's climate.

The Ross Ice Shelf: A History of Exploration and Scientific Discovery

The Ross Ice Shelf is one of the largest ice shelves in the world, covering an area of over 487,000 square kilometers. Located in the Ross Sea, off the coast of Antarctica, the ice shelf has been the focus of extensive exploration and scientific research over the past century. In this chapter, we will explore the history of the Ross Ice Shelf, and learn about the many discoveries and achievements that have been made through the study of this remarkable natural feature.

The Ross Ice Shelf was first discovered by the British explorer James Clark Ross in 1841, during his second Antarctic expedition. Ross was the first person to sail into the Ross Sea, and he named the ice shelf after his expedition sponsor, Sir James Clark. Despite this early discovery, however, it would be many years before the Ross Ice Shelf was fully explored and studied.

In the early 20th century, a number of explorers and scientists began to study the Ross Ice Shelf in more detail. In 1911, Robert Falcon Scott led an expedition to the Ross Sea, during which he discovered the Beardmore Glacier, a major feature of the Ross Ice Shelf. Later expeditions, led by Ernest Shackleton and others, further explored the Ross Ice Shelf and surrounding areas, making important discoveries and laying the groundwork for future scientific research.

One of the key scientific achievements related to the Ross Ice Shelf was the drilling of ice cores, which provide a record of ancient climate and environmental conditions. In the 1970s, an international team of scientists drilled a deep ice core from the Ross Ice Shelf, revealing a record of climate change stretching back thousands of years. This research has helped to deepen our understanding of the processes that shape our planet's climate, and has provided valuable insights into the history of the Antarctic region.

The Ross Ice Shelf has also been the site of a number of scientific research stations, which have been used to study a range of topics including geology, oceanography, and atmospheric science. These research stations have played an important role in advancing our understanding of the Ross Ice Shelf and the surrounding area, and have contributed to numerous important scientific discoveries over the years.

Despite the many achievements and discoveries made through the study of the Ross Ice Shelf, this unique natural feature remains a source of mystery and fascination for scientists and explorers alike. As we continue to study and explore the frozen continent of Antarctica, it is clear that the Ross Ice Shelf will continue to play an important role in our understanding of the planet's past, present, and future.

The Search for Meteorites in Antarctica: Studying the Origin of the Solar System

Antarctica is an important location for the study of meteorites, with over 20,000 meteorites discovered on the continent since the first discovery in 1912. The cold and dry environment of Antarctica provides an ideal setting for the preservation of meteorites, which can offer valuable insights into the formation and evolution of the solar system. In this chapter, we will explore the history of meteorite research in Antarctica, and learn about the many important discoveries that have been made through the study of these extraterrestrial rocks.

The first meteorite discovered in Antarctica was found by a Norwegian expedition in 1912, and since then numerous expeditions have been conducted to search for and study these rocks. One of the most significant of these expeditions was the US-led ANSMET program, which has been conducting meteorite searches in Antarctica since 1976. The ANSMET program has discovered thousands of meteorites, providing valuable insights into the composition and history of the solar system.

One of the key advantages of studying meteorites in Antarctica is the fact that the cold and dry environment helps to preserve these rocks in pristine condition. Many of the meteorites discovered in Antarctica are of types that are rare or even unknown on Earth, and their study has helped to advance our understanding of the processes that shaped the early solar system.

In addition to providing insights into the formation and evolution of the solar system, the study of meteorites in Antarctica has also shed light on the history of the Earth itself. For example, the discovery of a meteorite containing evidence of microbial life in 1984 raised the possibility that life may have originated elsewhere in the solar system and been brought to Earth via meteorites.

The study of meteorites in Antarctica is a fascinating and important field of research, with implications for our understanding of the history and evolution of the solar system and the origins of life on Earth. As we continue to explore and learn about this unique continent, it is clear that the search for meteorites will remain an important avenue for scientific discovery and exploration for many years to come.

Medieval Maps and the Idea of Terra Australis Incognita: The Imaginary Continent of the South

For centuries, maps of the world depicted a large, unknown landmass in the southern hemisphere known as Terra Australis Incognita, or the "unknown southern land." This imaginary continent, believed to be rich in resources and perhaps even inhabited by exotic creatures, was a fixture of medieval maps and a source of fascination for explorers and cartographers alike. In this chapter, we will explore the history of the idea of Terra Australis Incognita, and learn about the many ways in which this imaginary continent captured the imagination of people throughout the medieval period.

The idea of Terra Australis Incognita can be traced back to the ancient Greeks, who believed in the existence of a vast southern landmass that balanced out the continents of the northern hemisphere. However, it was during the medieval period that the idea of the unknown southern land began to take on a life of its own, appearing on maps and in works of literature and folklore.

One of the most famous depictions of Terra Australis Incognita is the Catalan Atlas, a 14th-century map produced in Catalonia, Spain. The map shows a large, vaguely defined landmass in the southern hemisphere, with labels indicating its supposed size and location. Other medieval maps, including the Ptolemaic maps of the 2nd century AD, also included depictions of a southern continent, albeit with varying degrees of accuracy and detail.

The idea of Terra Australis Incognita captured the imagination of medieval Europeans, who believed that this unknown continent was rich in resources and perhaps even home to exotic animals and civilizations. This belief was fueled by accounts of travelers and explorers who claimed to have seen or heard about the unknown southern land, as well as by works of literature and folklore that depicted the land as a place of mystery and adventure.

Despite the widespread belief in the existence of Terra Australis Incognita, the continent remained a mystery until the age of exploration in the 15th and 16th centuries. The discovery of Australia by Dutch explorers in 1606 shattered the myth of the unknown southern land, and paved the way for a new era of exploration and discovery in the southern hemisphere.

The idea of Terra Australis Incognita may have been nothing more than an imaginary construct, but it played an important role in shaping the imagination and worldview of people throughout the medieval period. As we continue to explore and learn about the history of maps and cartography, it is clear that the idea of the unknown southern land remains an important chapter in the story of human exploration and discovery.

The Piri Reis Map and the Mystery of Antarctica: Did Ancient Mariners Discover the Continent?

The Piri Reis Map is a 16th-century map that has long been the subject of controversy and speculation. The map, which shows the coastlines of Europe, Africa, and South America, also includes a depiction of a large landmass in the southern hemisphere that many believe to be Antarctica. If the map is accurate, it would suggest that ancient mariners may have discovered the frozen continent long before it was officially discovered by modern explorers. In this chapter, we will explore the mystery of the Piri Reis Map, and learn about the many theories and interpretations that have been put forward regarding its depiction of Antarctica.

The Piri Reis Map was created in 1513 by the Ottoman admiral and cartographer Piri Reis. The map was compiled from a variety of sources, including earlier maps and the accounts of travelers and explorers. While the accuracy of the map's depiction of the coastlines of Europe, Africa, and South America has been confirmed by modern scholars, its depiction of a southern continent has long been the subject of debate.

The landmass depicted on the Piri Reis Map has been interpreted by some as being Antarctica, and many have speculated that the map is evidence of ancient mariners having discovered the continent long before it was officially discovered in the modern era. However, the accuracy of this interpretation is hotly contested, with many scholars arguing that the landmass is more likely to be

South America or a distorted depiction of the southern tip of Africa.

Despite the controversy surrounding its depiction of Antarctica, the Piri Reis Map remains an important artifact in the history of cartography, and a source of fascination for scholars and the general public alike. The map's intricate details and sophisticated technique have led many to speculate about the possibility of ancient knowledge and exploration that have been lost to history.

The debate over the Piri Reis Map and its depiction of Antarctica is unlikely to be resolved anytime soon. However, the map serves as a reminder of the rich history of human exploration and discovery, and the many mysteries and unanswered questions that continue to captivate our imaginations. As we continue to explore and learn about our world, it is clear that there are still many unknowns waiting to be uncovered, and many stories waiting to be told.

Ancient Artifacts and Structures in Antarctica: Evidence of a Forgotten Civilization?

The idea of ancient civilizations in Antarctica has long been a subject of speculation and debate. While there is no concrete evidence to support the idea that a civilization once existed in Antarctica, there are some who believe that there may be clues in the form of ancient artifacts and structures that have been discovered on the continent. In this chapter, we will explore the evidence of ancient artifacts and structures in Antarctica, and examine the theories and speculations that have arisen in response.

One of the most intriguing discoveries in Antarctica is the so-called "Piri Reis map," which we explored in the previous chapter. While the map itself does not provide evidence of a lost civilization, some have speculated that the detailed knowledge of the continent's geography and topography displayed on the map could only have been possible if ancient mariners had explored the continent and mapped its features.

Other potential evidence of a lost civilization in Antarctica comes in the form of mysterious structures and artifacts that have been discovered on the continent. For example, in 1961, a team of geologists discovered a series of man-made stone structures near the coast of Antarctica. The structures, which resemble temples or other ceremonial buildings, have been the subject of much speculation and debate among researchers.

In addition to these structures, there have also been reports of other unusual artifacts and features in Antarctica, including mysterious pyramids and the remains of an ancient city. While these reports have yet to be confirmed, they continue to fuel speculation about the possibility of a lost civilization on the frozen continent.

Despite the intriguing nature of these discoveries, it is important to remember that the evidence for a lost civilization in Antarctica is highly speculative and lacking in concrete evidence. Many of the alleged structures and artifacts could be explained by natural phenomena, and there is no archaeological evidence to support the idea that a civilization ever existed on the continent.

As we continue to explore and learn about Antarctica, it is important to approach claims of ancient civilizations and lost cities with a healthy dose of skepticism. While the idea of a forgotten civilization on the frozen continent is an intriguing one, it is important to rely on evidence and scientific inquiry when evaluating such claims. Nevertheless, the mystery and speculation surrounding the possibility of an ancient civilization in Antarctica will continue to captivate the imaginations of people around the world, and inspire new stories and theories for years to come.

The History of Antarctic Fiction: From Edgar Allan Poe to John Carpenter

Antarctica has long been a popular setting for works of fiction, from the early days of polar exploration to the present day. In this chapter, we will explore the rich history of Antarctic fiction, and examine the many ways in which the frozen continent has inspired writers, filmmakers, and other artists throughout the years.

One of the earliest examples of Antarctic fiction is the novel "The Narrative of Arthur Gordon Pym of Nantucket" by Edgar Allan Poe, published in 1838. The novel tells the story of a young man who stows away on a whaling ship bound for the Antarctic, where he encounters a series of strange and terrifying events. The novel was highly influential in its day, and helped to establish Antarctica as a popular setting for works of fiction.

In the years that followed, numerous other writers and artists would explore the Antarctic setting in their works, including Jules Verne, H.P. Lovecraft, and Edgar Rice Burroughs. These early works often focused on the adventure and exploration aspects of the Antarctic setting, and helped to establish the frozen continent as a place of mystery and wonder.

In the mid-20th century, Antarctica began to feature more prominently in popular culture, with films like "The Thing from Another World" and "The Thing" (directed by John Carpenter) exploring the idea of extraterrestrial life and horror in the Antarctic setting. These works helped to cement Antarctica's place in the science fiction and horror genres, and inspired many other writers and filmmakers to explore the frozen continent in their own works.

In recent years, Antarctica has continued to inspire a wide range of fiction, including science fiction, horror, and adventure novels. Authors like Kim Stanley Robinson, James Rollins, and Dan Simmons have all used the Antarctic setting in their works, exploring themes of exploration, survival, and human adaptation in the harshest of environments.

Throughout its long history, Antarctic fiction has captivated readers and viewers around the world, offering a window into the mysteries and wonders of the frozen continent. From the early works of Edgar Allan Poe to the modern-day works of John Carpenter and beyond, the Antarctic setting has proven to be a fertile ground for imagination and creativity, and will no doubt continue to inspire new works of fiction for years to come.

The Future of Antarctica: Balancing Environmental Protection and Resource Development

As we approach the present day, the future of Antarctica is becoming an increasingly important topic of discussion and debate. With the continent serving as a crucial resource for scientific research, tourism, and potentially even resource development, it is important to consider the various challenges and opportunities that lie ahead. In this chapter, we will explore the future of Antarctica, and examine the ways in which we can balance environmental protection with resource development and other activities.

One of the most pressing issues facing Antarctica is climate change. The continent is experiencing some of the most dramatic impacts of global warming, including melting ice sheets, rising sea levels, and changing weather patterns. This has significant implications not only for the continent itself, but also for the rest of the world, as melting ice in Antarctica can contribute to rising sea levels and other environmental problems.

To address these challenges, it is important to prioritize environmental protection in Antarctica. This can be accomplished through a variety of measures, including protecting vulnerable ecosystems and wildlife, promoting sustainable tourism and research practices, and encouraging the use of renewable energy and other environmentally-friendly technologies.

At the same time, it is important to balance these environmental concerns with the potential benefits of resource development and other activities in Antarctica. The continent is home to a wealth of natural resources, including minerals, oil, and gas, that could be used to benefit human society. Additionally, the continent's unique geography and environment make it an ideal location for scientific research and exploration.

To ensure that these opportunities are realized in a responsible and sustainable manner, it is important to develop comprehensive policies and regulations for resource development and other activities in Antarctica. This can include measures such as environmental impact assessments, sustainable resource management practices, and international cooperation and coordination.

In addition to these challenges, the future of Antarctica will also be shaped by ongoing political and economic developments. As countries around the world continue to compete for resources and influence in the region, it will be important to balance these competing interests with the need for international cooperation and collaboration.

Ultimately, the future of Antarctica will be shaped by a variety of factors, including environmental concerns, resource development opportunities, political and economic developments, and more. By working together to address these challenges and opportunities in a responsible and sustainable manner, we can ensure that the frozen continent continues to serve as a valuable resource for scientific research, tourism, and more for generations to come.

Conclusion

As we come to the end of our journey through the history of Antarctica, it is clear that the frozen continent has played a crucial role in the history of human exploration, scientific discovery, and environmental conservation. From the early days of polar exploration to the present day, Antarctica has captured the imagination and inspired countless individuals to push the boundaries of human knowledge and experience.

One of the most remarkable aspects of Antarctica is its sheer remoteness and isolation. For much of human history, the continent remained a mysterious and unexplored region, known only through myth and legend. It was only with the advent of modern exploration that the true wonders of Antarctica began to be revealed.

Throughout the centuries, Antarctica has been the site of countless triumphs and tragedies. From the race to the South Pole to the heroic age of Antarctic exploration, brave men and women have braved the harsh conditions of the frozen continent in pursuit of scientific knowledge and personal achievement. These stories of endurance, courage, and perseverance continue to inspire us to this day.

At the same time, Antarctica has also been the site of some of the most pressing environmental challenges facing our planet. The continent's vulnerability to climate change, as well as the threats posed by resource development and other activities, highlight the need for continued vigilance and action to ensure that Antarctica remains a protected and sustainable environment.

Looking to the future, the challenges and opportunities facing Antarctica are numerous and complex. From the need to balance environmental protection with resource development to the ongoing geopolitical and economic developments in the region, there are many factors that will shape the continent's future.

Ultimately, the history of Antarctica is a testament to the resilience and adaptability of the human spirit. Despite the harsh conditions and remote location of the continent, humans have persevered and thrived in this frozen wilderness, building a legacy of scientific discovery and environmental protection that will continue to inspire generations to come.

As we reflect on the history of Antarctica, we are reminded of the importance of curiosity, exploration, and environmental stewardship. By continuing to push the boundaries of human knowledge and understanding, and by working together to protect the fragile ecosystems of the frozen continent, we can ensure that Antarctica remains a symbol of hope and inspiration for all of humanity.

Thank you for taking the time to read our book on the history of Antarctica. We hope that you found it engaging, informative, and inspiring.

If you enjoyed reading our book, we would appreciate it if you could take a moment to leave a positive review on the platform where you found it. Your review will help other readers discover our book and decide if it is the right fit for them.

Thank you again for your interest in the history of Antarctica, and we hope to see you again soon in our future publications.

Printed in Great Britain
by Amazon